A Finders' G

Rocks, Fossils and Soils

Written by Alison Milford

Contents

Collins

CW00847643

Earth's rocks, fossils and soils

Rocks make up a large part of
our planet. They're everywhere
– from mountains and cliffs
to rocks in rivers and deep
under the ground.

The Earth's outer layer that
we can see and feel is
made of solid rock.
It covers layers of deep
underground rock.
In the centre is a hot
liquid inner core.

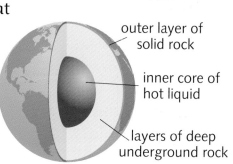

outer layer of
solid rock

inner core of
hot liquid

layers of deep
underground rock

Some rocks contain traces
of **ancient** creatures
and plants. These are
called fossils.

Soil is another important part of
our planet. It's **vital** for many plants
and living things to grow and survive.

Meet the experts

The best way to find out about rocks, fossils and soils is to visit different places to collect **samples** and take notes about them. This is called a field trip.

Experts who study rocks, fossils and soils often plan field trips for their investigations.

Geologists find out how rocks form and affect the earth.

Palaeontologists find out how fossilised creatures and plants lived long ago.

Soil scientists find out what soils contain and what can grow in them.

3

Field trip equipment

Before going on a field trip, experts:

- ask permission from the owners of the land
- check that it's safe
- pack the right equipment.

Rock or fossil field trip

- rucksack
- map
- newspaper for **delicate** samples
- tape measure
- camera
- plastic bags to put samples in
- labels and pen
- brushes
- rock hammer

- flat **chisels**
- hand lens to see details
- protective gloves, goggles, hard hat
- strong footwear

a rock hammer

flat head for breaking rocks

pointed end for digging and pulling

Soil field trip

Soil scientists have a similar equipment list apart from a few extra items.

- spades and trowels – useful for digging into the soil
- soil sieve – to separate soil from materials such as rocks and leaves
- soil core sample tool

Experts use field trip notebooks to take notes and draw pictures of what they see and find.

To get a section of soil, push the core sampler into the ground, then pull it out again.

Igneous rocks

Earth is covered in three types of rocks: igneous rocks, sedimentary rocks and metamorphic rocks.

Igneous rocks are the earth's most common rock and cover 95% of its surface.

The Giant's Causeway, in Northern Ireland, is made of columns of igneous rock called basalt. They were formed from cooled-down lava that came from a volcano over 50 million years ago.

How igneous rocks are formed

All igneous rocks start from a very hot liquid called magma which is deep under the earth's surface. Igneous rocks that cool on the earth's surface are called extrusive rocks. Igneous rocks that cool under the surface are called intrusive rocks.

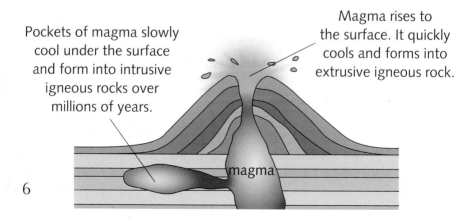

Pockets of magma slowly cool under the surface and form into intrusive igneous rocks over millions of years.

Magma rises to the surface. It quickly cools and forms into extrusive igneous rock.

magma

Intrusive and extrusive igneous rocks

Extrusive rocks have a fine **texture** because they don't contain many **crystals**. This is because the hot volcanic magma cools down too quickly for **minerals** to form. Basalt, rhyolite, obsidian and pumice are all extrusive rocks. They're soft and are often used as materials and ingredients for different things, such as road building and toothpaste, as well as making beautiful sculptures.

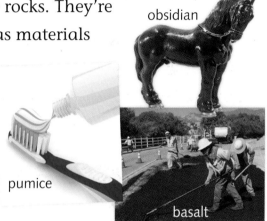

obsidian

pumice

basalt

Intrusive rocks have rougher textures because they contain lots of crystals. This is because the magma takes longer to cool down, allowing more crystals to form. Granite and diorite are intrusive rocks. They're hard-wearing and often used for buildings, bridges, statues and worktops.

Tower Bridge in London was built from granite that came from Cornwall.

7

Features of extrusive igneous rock

- *fine texture rocks*
- *quick cooling*
- *hardly any crystals*

These basalt rocks in Iceland are extrusive igneous rock. Basalt is also found on the moon!

Features of intrusive igneous rock

- *rough texture rocks*
- *slow cooling*
- *lots of crystals*

These granite rocks in Italy are intrusive igneous rock.

These rhyolite rocks in the USA are extrusive igneous rock.

These diorite rocks in the USA are intrusive igneous rock.

Igneous rock identification chart

A rock chart can help rock collectors work out what rock samples they've collected. This chart shows the differences in looks and texture between six intrusive and extrusive igneous rock samples.

Igneous rock	Sample	Texture	Look	Colours
Intrusive				
granite		rough	speckled with crystals slightly sparkly	white, pink, grey
diorite	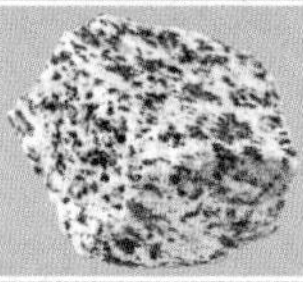	rough	speckled like salt and pepper	black, white
pegmatite	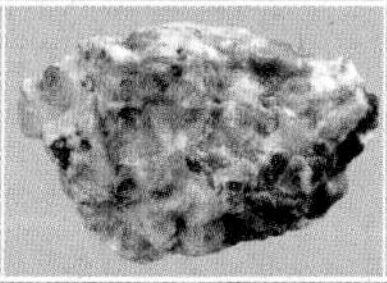	hard, sharp	**interlocking** crystals glassy	white, orange, black
Extrusive				
pumice	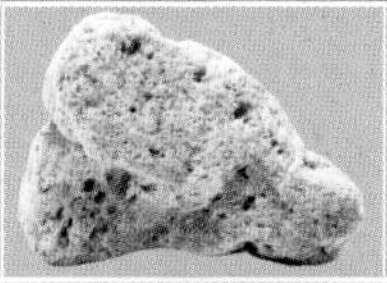	fine, light, crumbly	small holes bumpy	white, yellow, pink
basalt		fine	ridges white specks	grey, white specks
obsidian	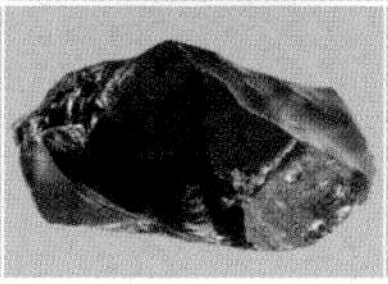	smooth	glassy, oblong	black

Sedimentary rocks

Sedimentary rocks aren't formed from hot magma like igneous rocks. They're layers of small rock fragments and other materials that have been **compressed** over a long time into solid rock.

How and where sedimentary rocks are formed

Sedimentary rocks can be found near water or in places where water once existed long ago.

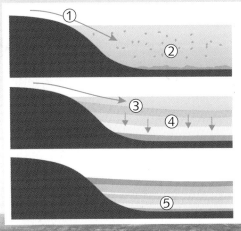

1. Small pieces of rock end up in the water.
2. Rock **sediments** settle on the water bed.
3. Over time, sediment lands on top of the last layer (called strata).
4. Top layers force the lower layers to **compact** tightly.
5. Minerals **cement** the layers into rock. Over time, sedimentary rocks appear.

The Grand Canyon, USA, is sedimentary rock.

Main types of sedimentary rocks

Sedimentary rocks can be sorted into different types depending on what materials are in them, what they look like and their texture. Use the table to find out about three main types of sedimentary rocks and their uses.

Field Notebook

Limestone
Main content: **calcium carbonate** *and compressed shells*
Uses: building materials, glass making
Look: yellowy white, fine-grained, layers, shells

Sandstone
Main content: compressed grains of sand
Uses: building materials, tiles, household pots, sculptures
Look: reddish brown, medium-grained, rough grains

Coal
Main content: compressed swamp plants
Uses: fuel for heat used in homes and for powering machines
Look: brown layers, shiny on top, medium-grained

11

What are fossils?

The layers in sedimentary rocks not only contain small rock sediments, they also contain the remains of plants and creatures that lived long ago. These are called fossils.

Many fossils are of living things that have become **extinct**, such as the dinosaurs. Studying fossils help us find out what they looked like, how they lived and where they lived.

Lots of fossils have been found in the layered limestone cliffs at Bridport in Dorset, UK.

How fossils are formed

Most fossils are formed in one of three ways.

1. Fossils are formed when something is compressed tightly in sedimentary rock.

A living thing dies near or in water.

It decays and is covered in sediment.

Rock minerals harden in the bones' shape and become rock.

The fossil is compacted into the sedimentary rock layer.

2. Small animals like insects become fossils when they are covered and **preserved** in **amber**, a **resin** that comes from trees.

13

3. Fossils are formed when plants and soft parts of creatures die, and an outline of their shape is left in the rock.

Experts can discover lots of things about these ancient animals and plants from their fossils.

Fossil	Living thing	Time	Notes
trilobite		extinct 500 million years ago	oval shaped long spine thick shell lived under the sea fed on plankton
crinoid sea lily		extinct 500 million years ago	looked like a flower main body at top of stem long arms lived deep on ocean floors similar types still exist
percomorph fish		extinct 95 million years ago	bony fish predator of small fish 3.5 centimetres long large mouth forked fin tail

Fossil	Living thing	Time	Notes
ichthyosaur		extinct 250 million years ago	sea predator of small fish flippers pointed head and snout long vertical tail two to four metres in length
splay-footed cricket		extinct 140 million years ago	large body sandy habitat large paddle-like feet parts predator similar crickets exist
pterodactyl		extinct 150 million years ago	winged reptile swampy wetland habitat one metre wingspan long beak with 90 teeth ate fish

Metamorphic rocks

Metamorphic rocks wouldn't exist without igneous and sedimentary rocks. Metamorphic means "to change", and metamorphic rocks are igneous and sedimentary rocks that have gone through an amazing change.

The light layers in these mountains in Norway are metamorphic rock.

Metamorphic rocks are formed deep under the earth's surface where the magma is extremely hot. This magma heat and the immense underground **pressure** of vast moving rocks can make some igneous and sedimentary rocks totally change in shape and texture.

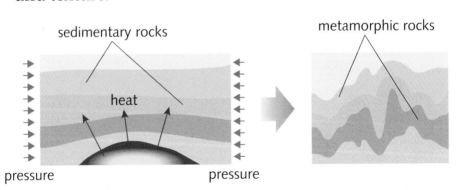

sedimentary rocks

heat

pressure

pressure

metamorphic rocks

These changed rocks become metamorphic rocks. They can look stripy and uneven as if they've been tightly squeezed and twisted.

Marble

Marble is the most common metamorphic rock. It takes millions of years of heat and pressure for marble to be formed.

Field Notebook

Origins: limestone

Look: white, hard surface, crystals, shiny, bumpy

Marble is often used for building materials, monuments and sculptures.

This polished marble shows its metamorphic wavy twisted layers.

The Taj Mahal in India is built from white marble.

17

Rock weathering and erosion

Rocks are changing all the time. Two of these changes are due to weathering and erosion.

Weathering

Weathering happens when rocks are slowly worn down or broken into smaller pieces from extreme weather, water, movement of rocks, or plants growing by them.

Erosion

Small rocks that have become loose from weathered rocks can be moved to other places. This is often done by the wind, by water or by falling away due to the weakness in the main rock. This movement of rocks is called erosion.

rock cracked from ice pushing it open

These smooth pebbles have been worn down as they have been transported and bashed about by the sea.

18

The rock cycle

Over time, igneous, sedimentary and metamorphic rocks can change from one type of rock to another. This is called the rock cycle. It makes and recycles rocks.

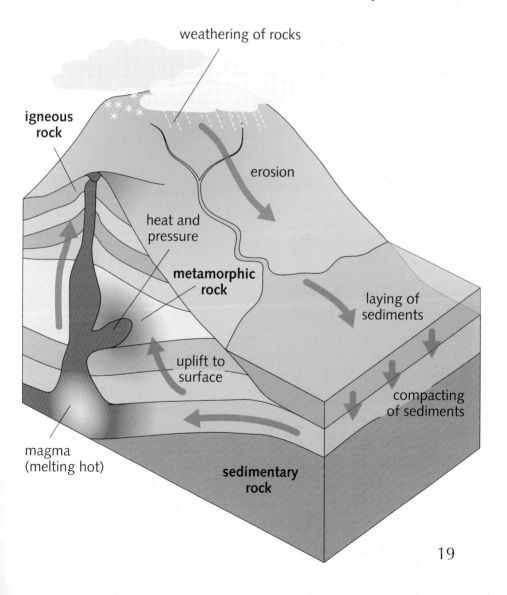

weathering of rocks

igneous rock

erosion

heat and pressure

metamorphic rock

laying of sediments

uplift to surface

compacting of sediments

magma (melting hot)

sedimentary rock

Soil

What is soil?

Soil forms when weathered
rock is broken down and
mixes with other ground materials
such as **decaying** plants and animals.

These materials are covered by more
layers of the same **organic material** and rocks.
Water and air help bind the layers together.

Soil can take millions of years
to form and is a process that
goes on every day. It plays
a vital part in supporting and
balancing life on Earth.

Soil can help plants grow,
support creatures and
balance our climate.

Soil layers

Soil is mainly made up of five different layers.

The very top layer is often dark brown due to the decaying **organisms** in the soil. The rich **nutrients** from these help plants grow.

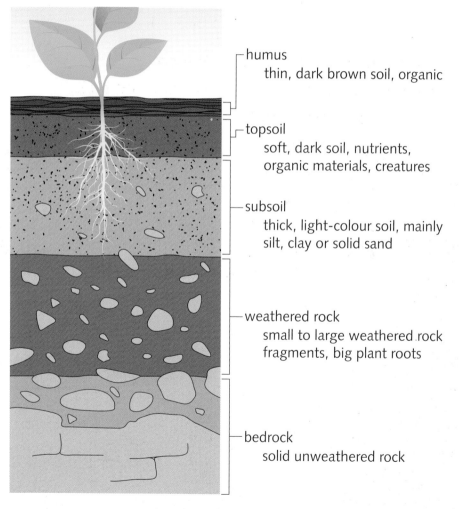

humus
thin, dark brown soil, organic

topsoil
soft, dark soil, nutrients, organic materials, creatures

subsoil
thick, light-colour soil, mainly silt, clay or solid sand

weathered rock
small to large weathered rock fragments, big plant roots

bedrock
solid unweathered rock

Different types of soils

There are three main types of soil: clay, sand and silt. Most soils have a mix of these three types.

The way soil is formed depends on several things:

1. Type of weathered rock

2. Land forms – flat land has deeper layers; high land has shallow layers

3. Climate – hot, cold, wet, dry

4. Types of organisms in the soil.

Soil scientists take a soil sample to find out what type of soil it is. They ask questions about the soil to help them decide.

Field Notebook

Location: _____   Climate: _____

What colour is it?   What does it smell like?   What does it contain?

What does it feel like?   What living things are in it?

22

Soil type chart

This chart tells us what the three main soil types look like, feel like, whether they are good for plants and how well water drains through them.

hand lens used to look at soil closely

Soil	Look	Texture	Drainage/growth
clay	brown, blue, grey, red	sticky, thick, heavy, small particles	bad drainage, bad plant growth
sand	white to dark yellow	fine-grain, light, large particles	good drainage, prone to dryness, bad plant growth
silt	light to dark brown	soft, smooth, medium particles	good drainage, good plant growth

Soil uses

Plants need soil to grow. Very **fertile** soils produce many plants compared to very dry or waterlogged soils.

Farming

Farmers rely on good soil to grow crops. In places where the soil is weak, extra humus rich with nutrients is added to the topsoil.

Some farmers give areas of soil a break from growing so that it can rebuild its nutrients.

Natural uses

Rain or floodwater is **absorbed** deep into the soil to feed plants or to travel underground to streams and rivers. Soil with lots of sand in it can help stop flooding because rainwater can drain through it easily. Soil with lots of heavy clay in it floods more easily because rainwater can't drain through it.

Soil as a home

Birds, snakes and mini-beasts all
make their home in the soil, as
well as rabbits, mice and moles,
who dig burrows deep into the earth.

If you dig into the soil, it doesn't take long to find
a worm in it. Worms can improve our soil by just
eating it. The leftover soil that comes out the other end
of the worm is rich and full of nutrients.

Human uses

Apart from growing plants and
food, we use soil for making
many things, such as clay
pots, dried soil bricks
for buildings and for
road foundations.

After the field trips

After the field trips, any samples and information are taken back to study in more detail. The field notebooks and charts help remind the experts what they've discovered.

Labelled rock and fossil samples are carefully unwrapped and placed under a microscope to be looked at in more detail.

A soil sample can be tested for a range of things such as:

- water **retention**
- other types of soils within it
- **microscopic** details of organic materials
- its age
- what would grow in it.

Rocks, fossils and soils are a major part of our planet. They hold clues to how it was formed in the past and how it's forming today.

By looking at them in more detail, we can gain a better understanding about their importance and how our Earth works.

Perhaps one day, you'll be a rock, fossil or soil expert and discover more about what rocks, fossils and soils can tell us about planet Earth.

Glossary

absorbed   soaked up or taken in a liquid such as water

amber   hard, clear, yellow fossil of very old tree resin

ancient   very old

calcium carbonate   white salt powder often found in chalk and limestone

cement   join and glue together

chisels   tools with sharp edges that cut and shape rocks

compact   tightly pack together

compressed   pressed or squeezed into a small space

crystals   hard, clear type of mineral found in rocks

decaying   slowly rotting away

delicate   fragile and easily broken

extinct   when something no longer exists

fertile   good land or soil that can grow many plants

interlocking   two or more things joined together

microscopic   very small; can only be seen clearly with a microscope

minerals   solids (such as crystals) that are formed underground

nutrients   vitamins, minerals and other elements that help things grow

organic material   a mix of dead plants and animals and animal body waste such as cow poo (manure)

organisms living things such as plants or living creatures

preserved   something that has been kept in good condition

pressure   a build-up of weight or force pushing against something

28

resin a yellowy, brown sticky liquid from a tree

retention to keep or hold something, such as holding water

samples small examples of things that can tell us information about them

sediments materials such as sand and stone that fall to the bottom of a liquid such as water

texture the feel of something

vital very important and needed

Index

rock finder

igneous rocks

sedimentary rocks

metamorphic rocks

fossil finder

compression in sedimentary rock

preserved in amber

soil finder

soil uses

31

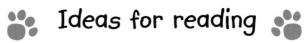

Ideas for reading

Written by Clare Dowdall, PhD
Lecturer and Primary Literacy Consultant

Reading objectives:
- retrieve and record information from non-fiction
- discuss their understanding and explain the meaning of words in context
- draw inferences and justify these with evidence
- identify main ideas drawn from more than one paragraph and summarise ideas

Spoken language objectives:
- participate in discussions, presentations, performances, role play, improvisations and debates

Curriculum links: Science – Rocks; Geography – Natural resources

Resources: jar of soil from the school grounds, paper and pens, ICT

Build a context for reading

- Look at some soil from the school grounds in a glass jar. Ask children to describe what they can see and suggest how it has been formed.
- Explain that you are going to become rock, fossil and soil experts. Show children the book. Read the blurb together.
- Ask if any children have been on field trips, and to share their experiences.

Understand and apply reading strategies

- Turn to pp2–3. Read aloud and check children's understanding by asking them to explain interesting vocabulary, e.g. what is a *liquid inner core?* What is it like at the centre of the earth?
- Ask children to read pp4–5 to themselves. Discuss what each piece of equipment is used for on rock, fossil and soil field trips.